curious about

VALENTINE'S DAY

BY ELIZABETH KASSUELKE

AMICUS LEARNING

What are you

CHAPTER ONE

Spread the Love
PAGE
4

CHAPTER TWO

The History of Valentine's Day
PAGE
10

curious about?

CHAPTER THREE

Let's Celebrate!
PAGE **16**

Stay Curious! Learn More 22
Glossary. 24
Index 24

Curious About is published by
Amicus Learning, an imprint of Amicus
P.O. Box 227, Mankato, MN 56002
www.amicuspublishing.us

Copyright © 2026 Amicus.
International copyright reserved in all countries.
No part of this book may be reproduced in any
form without written permission from the publisher.

Editor: Ana Brauer
Series Designer: Kathleen Petelinsek
Book Designer and Photo Researcher: Sara Hood

Library of Congress Cataloging-in-Publication Data
Names: Kassuelke, Elizabeth author
Title: Curious about Valentine's Day / by Elizabeth Kassuelke.
Description: Mankato, MN : Amicus Learning, [2026]
| Series: Curious about holidays | Includes bibliographical
references and index. | Audience: Ages 6–9 | Audience:
Grades 2–3 | Summary: "Why do we celebrate Valentine's
Day? Learn about the history, significance, and celebrations
of Valentine's Day in this question-and-answer book for
elementary-aged readers. Includes table of contents, glossary,
further resources, and index"— Provided by publisher.
Identifiers: LCCN 2025014052 (print) | LCCN 2025014053
(ebook) | ISBN 9798892008525 library binding | ISBN
9798892009188 paperback | ISBN 9798892009843 ebook
Subjects: LCSH: Valentine's Day—Juvenile literature
Classification: LCC GT4925 .K37 2026 (print) | LCC GT4925
(ebook) | DDC 394.2618—dc23/eng/20250518
LC record available at https://lccn.loc.gov/2025014052
LC ebook record available at https://lccn.loc.gov/2025014053

Photo Credits: Getty Images/Alexander Spatari, 17 (top, right),
17 (bottom, right), Anastasiia Krivenok, 21, Jeremy Walker, 17
(top, left), Jupiterimages, 9, lisegagne, 5, LPETTET, 18–19, O2O
Creative, 12–13, Pakin Songmor, 15 (bottom), Peter Dazeley,
15 (second from top), Rouelle Umali/Xinhua News Agency,
16, RUBEN BONILLA GONZALO, 15 (middle), StephePhoto,
15 (top), Svetlana Repnitskaya, 2, 6–7, @ Didier Marti, 17
(bottom, left); Shutterstock/Evgeny Atamanenko, 14, Pixel-Shot,
cover, 1, Prostock-studio, 3, 20, 15 (second from bottom),
SeventyFour, 8; The Noun Project/Kholifah, 22, 23, metami
septiana, 22, 23; Wikimedia Commons/Maxfield Parrish, 2,10

Every effort has been made to contact copyright holders for
material reproduced in this book. Any omissions will be rectified
in subsequent printings if notice is given to the publisher.

Printed in United States of America

CHAPTER ONE

What is Valentine's Day about?

Valentine's Day is about showing love! You might get flowers and chocolates. Or you might get a card. Adults might go on a date. At school, you might celebrate with treats! How sweet!

Valentine's Day is celebrated on February 14 every year.

SPREAD THE LOVE

5

SPREAD THE LOVE

People all over the world celebrate Valentine's Day.

Who celebrates Valentine's Day?

DID YOU KNOW?
Cupid is a **symbol** of Valentine's Day. He is the Roman god of love.

Everyone can! A lot of people celebrate **romance**. But Valentine's Day is for all types of love. Show your parents or siblings you love them. You can also celebrate with your friends and teachers. Show yourself some love, too!

Valentine's Day is a day to say "I love you."

What does it mean to be someone's valentine?

SPREAD THE LOVE

It means you are special to them! Anyone could be your valentine. You could ask your mom or dad. You could ask a friend. Some might ask their crush to be their valentine. You might get a greeting card, candy, or a **poem**.

Saying "Be my Valentine" is a way to tell someone you like them.

SPREAD THE LOVE

CHAPTER 2

HISTORY OF VALENTINE'S DAY

Valentine's Day is named after **Saint** Valentine.

Who invented Valentine's Day?

There are many stories! We're not sure what's true. But we know it has something to do Saint Valentine. Saint Valentine was a Roman priest in the third century. He married couples against the king's law. This made him the saint of love.

DID YOU KNOW?
Some stories say Saint Valentine wrote "From your Valentine" in his letters. That might be why we call people valentines today.

Why do we write poems on Valentine's Day?

An English author named Geoffrey Chaucer wrote a poem in the 1300s. It said Saint Valentine's Day was the day birds choose a **mate**. Chaucer's poem inspired people to celebrate love on Valentine's Day.

Writing a poem is a fun way to tell someone you love them.

Why do we give people cards on Valentine's Day?

Handmade cards show love and kindness.

They make spreading love easy! Valentine's Day is a good day for love letters. People have done this for many years. When printing was invented in the 1400s, people started making cards for their loved ones.

1 CANDY

2 GREETING CARD

3 FLOWERS

4 DATE NIGHT

5 JEWELRY

POPULAR VALENTINE'S DAY GIFTS

CHAPTER THREE

Do other countries celebrate Valentine's Day?

LET'S CELEBRATE!

Many couples get married together in one big ceremony in the Philippines.

Yes! But each country celebrates differently. Mexico celebrates the "Day of Love and Friendship." The Philippines holds mass weddings for many couples to get married at once. In Japan, you might receive a "true love chocolate."

DAYS OF LOVE AROUND THE WORLD

BRAZIL
Lovers' Day
June 12

CZECH REPUBLIC
Day of Love
May 1

ARGENTINA
Sweetness Week
July 1–7

WALES
St. Dwynwen's Day
January 25

LET'S CELEBRATE!

Making cookies is a fun Valentine's Day activity.

How can I celebrate?

Cut hearts out of construction paper. You can use them to decorate a room. Get out some markers and make a homemade card. You could bake heart-shaped cookies. Grab your family and watch a sweet movie.

How can I show love on Valentine's Day?

LET'S CELEBRATE!

You can show love with hugs or kind words.

There are many ways to show you love someone! You could write them a note. Or give them a card. You could gift them some flowers or something sweet. You could give them a hug. Or tell them they're special!

Valentine's Day is a time to spread love in your own special way.

DID YOU KNOW?
Teachers receive more Valentine's Day cards than anyone else.

LET'S CELEBRATE!

STAY CURIOUS!

ASK MORE QUESTIONS

What's the story behind Cupid?

Why do we give out candy on Valentine's Day?

Try a BIG QUESTION: Why should we show people we love them?

SEARCH FOR ANSWERS

Search the library catalog or the Internet.
A librarian, teacher, or parent can help you.

Using Keywords
Find the looking glass.

Keywords are the most important words in your question.

If you want to know about:
- the story of Cupid, type: CUPID AND VALENTINE'S DAY
- why we give out candy on Valentine's Day, type: CANDY AND VALENTINE'S DAY

LEARN MORE

FIND GOOD SOURCES

Here are some good, safe sources you can use in your research. Your librarian can help you find more.

Books

Make Your Own Valentine's Day Crafts by Kayla Rossow, 2025.

Valentine's Day by Steve Foxe, 2024.

Internet Sites

Britannica Kids: Valentine's Day
https://kids.britannica.com/kids/article/Valentines-Day/390980
Britannica is an encyclopedia with educational information on many topics.

National Geographic Kids: Valentine's Day
https://kids.nationalgeographic.com/celebrations/article/valentines-day
National Geographic Kids is an educational website for kids.

Every effort has been made to ensure that these websites are appropriate for children. However, because of the nature of the Internet, it's impossible to guarantee that these sites will remain active indefinitely or that their contents will not be altered.

SHARE AND TAKE ACTION

With an adult, make cookies and share them with your teachers and classmates.

Write a letter to someone telling them how much you love them.

Spread kindness by holding the door or sharing a smile.

GLOSSARY

mate A pair of animals that live or have offspring together.

poem A piece of writing, often with words that rhyme and have rhythm.

romance A feeling of excitement and mystery associated with love.

saint A person acknowledged as holy and typically regarded as being in heaven after death.

symbol A sign, shape, or object that stands for something else.

INDEX

candy, 8, 15
cards, 4, 8, 14, 19, 20, 21
Chaucer, Geoffrey, 13
chocolates, 4, 17
cookies, 18, 19
Cupid, 7
friends, 7, 8, 17
Philippines, 16, 17
poems, 8, 12–13
printing, 14
Saint Valentine, 10–11

About the Author

Elizabeth Kassuelke is a Creative Writing MFA student at Minnesota State University, Mankato. She is passionate about education. She loves writing and certainly loves love.